551.5   Mann, Rachel,
MAN   1975-

C₁   Sun and rain.

                              34880030019975
$13.26

Sun and Rain

by Rachel Mann

Reading Consultant: Wiley Blevins, M.A.
Phonics/Early Reading Specialist

COMPASS POINT BOOKS

Minneapolis, Minnesota

Compass Point Books
3109 West 50th Street, #115
Minneapolis, MN 55410

Visit Compass Point Books on the Internet at *www.compasspointbooks.com*
or e-mail your request to *custserv@compasspointbooks.com*

Photographs ©: Cover: Index Stock/Omni Photo Communications, Inc., p. 1: Index Stock/Omni Photo Communications, Inc., p. 6: Bruce Coleman, Inc./Danilo Donadoni, p. 7: Minden Pictures/Konrad Wothe, p. 8: Corbis/A. & J. Verkaik, p. 9: Jeffrey Rich Nature Photography, p. 10: Corbis/Roy Morse, p. 11: Index Stock/Omni Photo Communications, Inc., p. 12: Top: BananaStock, p. 12: Bottom: DigitalVision

Editorial Development: Alice Dickstein, Alice Boynton
Photo Researcher: Wanda Winch
Design/Page Production: Silver Editions, Inc.

Library of Congress Cataloging-in-Publication Data
Mann, Rachel, 1975-
  Sun and rain / by Rachel Mann.
     p. cm. — (Compass Point phonics readers)
Summary: Shows benefits of sun and rain in an easy-to-read text that
incorporates phonics instruction and rebuses.
  ISBN 0-7565-0525-9 (hardcover : alk. paper)
  1. Sunshine—Juvenile literature. 2. Rain—Juvenile literature. 3.
Reading—Phonetic method—Juvenile literature. [1. Sunshine. 2. Rain. 3.
Reading—Phonetic method. 4. Rebuses.] I. Title. II. Series.
  QB521.5.M36 2004
  551.5'271—dc21   2003006370

Table of Contents

Dear Parent or Caregiver,

Welcome to Compass Point Phonics Readers, books of information for young children. Each book concentrates on specific phonic sounds and words commonly found in beginning reading materials. Featuring eye-catching photographs, every book explores a single science or social studies concept that is sure to grab a child's interest.

So snuggle up with your child, and let's begin. Start by reading aloud the Mother Goose nursery rhyme on the next page. As you read, stress the words in dark type. These are the words that contain the phonic sounds featured in this book. After several readings, pause before the rhyming words, and let your child chime in.

Now let's read *Sun and Rain*. If your child is a beginning reader, have him or her first read it silently. Then ask your child to read it aloud. For children who are not yet reading, read the book aloud as you run your finger under the words. Ask your child to imitate, or "echo," what he or she has just heard.

Discussing the book's content with your child:
Explain to your child that clouds are made up of many tiny drops of water. The tiny drops join and make large drops. As the drops get larger and larger, they become heavier and heavier. When they get too heavy, they fall as rain.

At the back of the book is a fun Tic-Tac-Toe game. Your child will take pride in demonstrating his or her mastery of the phonic sounds and the high-frequency words.

Enjoy Compass Point Phonics Readers and watch your child read and learn!

4

A Well

As round as an apple,
As deep as a **cup**
All the kings horses,
Can't fill it **up.**

The big yellow sun is up.
It makes us warm.

The sun helps plants.
Its light helps plants grow.

Rain clouds block the sun.
Drip! Drip! Drop!

Ponds fill up.
Ducks and bugs drink.

Grass and [flowers] get wet.
Rain helps them grow.

It is hot and windy.
The big yellow sun is back.

Tell what the weather is.

Word List

Short *u*
bugs
ducks
sun
up
us

l-Blends
block
plants

High-Frequency
drink
light
them
warm

Science
rain
weather
windy

Tic-Tac-Toe

You will need:
- 5 game pieces for each player, such as 5 pennies and 5 checkers

Game 1

up	plants	black
drink	them	us
ducks	cut	mud

How to Play

- Players take turns reading aloud a word and then covering it with a game piece.
- The first player to cover 3 words in a row down, across, or on the diagonal wins.
- After playing Game 1, the players can go to Game 2.

Game 2

bugs	warm	truck
sun	bus	class
block	hug	light

Read More

Blackaby, Susan. *Green and Growing: A Book about Plants.* Minneapolis, Minn.: Picture Window Books, 2003.

Flanagan, Alice K. *Weather.* Minneapolis, Minn.: Compass Point Books, 2001.

Frost, Helen. *We Need Water.* Mankato, Minn.: Pebble Books, 2000.

Index